797,885 Books
are available to read at

Forgotten Books

www.ForgottenBooks.com

Forgotten Books' App
Available for mobile, tablet & eReader

ISBN 978-1-332-04971-4
PIBN 10276165

This book is a reproduction of an important historical work. Forgotten Books uses state-of-the-art technology to digitally reconstruct the work, preserving the original format whilst repairing imperfections present in the aged copy. In rare cases, an imperfection in the original, such as a blemish or missing page, may be replicated in our edition. We do, however, repair the vast majority of imperfections successfully; any imperfections that remain are intentionally left to preserve the state of such historical works.

Forgotten Books is a registered trademark of FB &c Ltd.
Copyright © 2015 FB &c Ltd.
FB &c Ltd, Dalton House, 60 Windsor Avenue, London, SW19 2RR.
Company number 08720141. Registered in England and Wales.

For support please visit www.forgottenbooks.com

1 MONTH OF FREE READING

at

www.ForgottenBooks.com

By purchasing this book you are eligible for one month membership to ForgottenBooks.com, giving you unlimited access to our entire collection of over 700,000 titles via our web site and mobile apps.

To claim your free month visit:
www.forgottenbooks.com/free276165

* Offer is valid for 45 days from date of purchase. Terms and conditions apply.

English
Français
Deutsche
Italiano
Español
Português

www.forgottenbooks.com

Mythology Photography **Fiction** Fishing Christianity **Art** Cooking Essays Buddhism Freemasonry Medicine **Biology** Music **Ancient Egypt** Evolution Carpentry Physics Dance Geology **Mathematics** Fitness Shakespeare **Folklore** Yoga Marketing **Confidence** Immortality Biographies Poetry **Psychology** Witchcraft Electronics Chemistry History **Law** Accounting **Philosophy** Anthropology Alchemy Drama Quantum Mechanics Atheism Sexual Health **Ancient History Entrepreneurship** Languages Sport Paleontology Needlework Islam **Metaphysics** Investment Archaeology Parenting Statistics Criminology **Motivational**

F 179.20.1

Berners. A treatyse o
wyth an angle. 188

HARVARD COLLEGE LIBRARY

A Treatyse of Fysshynge with an Angle.

Bibliotheca Curiosa.

A Treatyse of Fysshynge wyth an Angle,

BY
DAME JULIANA BERNERS.

Originally Printed by Wynkyn de Worde in 1496.

Edited by
"PISCATOR."

PRIVATELY PRINTED, EDINBURGH.

1885.

9.20.1 ✓

HARVARD UNIVERSITY LIBRARY

*This edition is limited to 275 small-paper copies,
and 75 large-paper copies.*

Introduction.

THE Work here reprinted is universally regarded as being the first English book on Angling, and must, therefore, ever be interesting, not only to the brethren of the gentle craft, but also to the lover of our old English literature, even though he has never cast a fly, or so much as watched a float.

An excellent Bibliographical notice of the work has appeared in the Library Chronicle, from the pen of Mr. WILLIAM E. A. AXON, and to it I am indebted for the following particulars.

The supposed authoress was a lady named Juliana Barnes or Berners, born towards the end of the fourteenth century at Roding-Berners, in the Hundred of Dunmow, Essex. Her father was Sir James Berners, who was beheaded in 1388, as one of the evil advisers of Richard II. She is said to have been Prioress of Sopwell Nunnery in Hertfordshire, a dependancy of the Abbey of St. Albans. To this nun is attributed the "Book of St. Albans," the earliest sporting work in the language! As Mr. Axon says, "she may have gained the experience that would furnish material for her writings before she took the veil." The book obtains its name from having been printed at St. Albans in 1486 by that unknown printer, who is generally styled "The Schoolmaster of St. Albans." It is divided into three parts: the first part treats of Hawking, the second of Hunting, and the third of Coat-armour. In 1496, Wynkyn de Worde issued a second edition of "The Book of St. Albans," adding a fourth part, the "Treatyse of Fysshynge."

The claim of Juliana Berners to the authorship of the first part rests principally on the closing lines of the discourse on Hunting, which ends thus:—

> Your playe for to wynne or that you come inne,
> Explicit Dam Julyans Barnes in her boke of
> Huntyng.

As regards the Treatyse of Fysshynge, the evidence is more shadowy still; it rests, according to Mr. Van Siclen,* on the ungallant hypothesis that only a woman could have given such directions for making a rod, and that no man could have been guilty of so "delightful a *non sequitur* in many of the arguments."

Those interested in early Angling Literature should compare the instructions given by Dame Berners with those of John Davies, in his "Secrets of Angling," originally printed in 1613. See "Bibliotheca Curiosa," No. 43.)

---

* Who edited an American reprint in 1875, 12mo.

Introduction. vii

BIBLIOGRAPHY OF THE TREATYSE OF FYSSHYNGE.

(a.) *Forming part of the Book of St. Albans.*

1.	*Westminster, 1496.	Emprynted by Wynkyn de Worde. Fo. Black Letter.
2.	†London (no date).	Imprynted . . . by Wynkyn de Worde. pp. 92. 4to. Black Letter.
3.	London (no date).	Imprynted . . . by Wylliam Coplande. pp. 96. 4to. Bl. Let.
4.	‡London (no date).	Imprynted . . . by Wylliam Coplande. pp. 96. 4to. Bl. Let.
5.	§London (no date).	*First Part*, Imprynted . . . by Robert Foye. Parts 2 and 3, Imprynted . . . by Wylliam Copland. pp. 96. 4to. Bl. Let.
6.	London (no date).	Imprynted in the Vyentre . . . by Wylliam Copland. pp. 96. 4to. Black Letter.
7.	‖ London (no date).	Imprynted .. by Wyllyam Powell. pp. 96. 4to. Black Letter.
8.	Lond. (no date).	Imprynted . . . by Ab. Vele.
9.	London, 1586.	Printed by Edward Allde. pp. 88. 4to. Black Letter.

* Copies on vellum are in the Pembroke and Grenville collections, and on paper in the British Museum and Bodleian libraries.—Sold: White Knights, £60, 18s.; Haworth, £39, 18s.

† The only copy known is in the Huth Library.

‡ Each Part has a distinct colophon.

§ Sold, Dent, £10. 10s.

‖ Sold, Haworth, £7, 5s.—Editions by Copland in 1548, 1551, 1553, 1554, 1561, 1568, and 1569; by

Introduction.

10.	London, 1614.	Entitled "A jewell for Gentrie."
11.	London, 1810.	Edited by Haslewood. 8vo.

(b.) As a separate Pamphlet.

1.	*London (no date).	Imprynted ... by Wynkyn de Worde. 4to. Bl. Let.
2.	London, 1590.	Printed by John Wolfe. 4to.
3.	London, 1596.	Printed by John Wolfe. 4to.
4.	London, 1600.	Printed by John Wolfe. 4to.
5.	London, 1606.	Printed by John Wolfe. 4to.
6.	London, 1827.	Printed by Baskerville. 8vo.
7.	London, 1880.	Edited by Rev. M. G. Watkins. Reprinted in facsimile. 4to.
8.	†London, 1883.	With Preface and Glossary, by William Satchell, 4to.
9.	Edinburgh, 1885.	The present edition. 8vo.

Henry Tab (no date); by John Waley in 1546 an 1586; and by Powell in 1547, 1550, 1567.

* Signatures A to P iiij.

† Only 200 copies printed.—An older form of the Treatyse, from an MS. belonging to Alfred Denison, Esq., was issued, under the same date, by Mr. Satchell.

Here begynnyth the treatyse of fysshynge wyth an Angle.

SALAMON in his parablys sayth that a good spyryte makyth a flourynge aege, that is a fayre aege and a longe. And syth it is soo: I aske this questyon. Whiche ben the meanes and the causes that enduce a man into a mery spyryte: Truly to my beste dyscrecion it semeth good dysportes and honest gamys in whom a man Ioyeth wythout ony repentannce after. Thenne folowyth it ye gode dysportes and honest games ben cause of mannys fayr aege and longe life. And therfore now woll I chose of foure good dysportes and honeste gamys, that is to wyte: of huntynge: hawkynge: fysshynge: and foulynge. The beste to my symple dyscrecion why then is fysshynge: callyd Anglynge wyth a rodde: and a lyne and an hoke, And therof to treate as my symple wytte may suffyce: both for the sayd reason of Salamon and also for the reason that phisyk makyth in this wyse *(Si tibi deficiant medici medice tibi fiant : hæc tria mens leta labor et moderata dieta).*

Ye shall vnderstande that this is for to saye, Yf a man lacke leche or medicyne he shall make thre thynges his leche and medycyne: and he shall nede neuer no moo. The fyrste of theym is a mery thought. The second is labour not outraged. The thyrde is dyete mesurable. Fyrste that yf a man wyll euer more be in mery thoughtes and haue a gladde spyryte: he must eschewe all contraryous company and all places of debate where he myghte haue ony occasyons of malencoly. And yf he woll haue a labour not outrageous he muste thenne ordeyne him to his hertys ease and pleasaunce wythout studye pensyfnesse or traueyle a mery occupacyon whyche may reioyce his herte: and in whyche his spyrytes may haue a mery delyte. And yf he woll be dyetyd mesurably he must eschewe all places of ryotte whyche is cause of surfette and of syknesse, And he must drawe him to places of swete ayre and hungry: And ete nourishable meetes and dyffyable also.

TREATYSE OF FYSSHYNGE.

NOW thenne woll I descryue the sayd dysportes and gamys to finde the beste of theym as veryly as I can, alle be it that the ryght noble and full worthy prynce the duke of Yorke late callid mayster of game hath discryued the myrthes of huntynge lyke as I thynke to dyscryue of it and of alle the other. For huntynge as to myn entent is to laboryous, For the hunter must alwaye renne and folowe his houndes: traueyllynge and swetynge full sore. He blowyth tyll his lyppes blyster And whan he wenyth it be an hare full oft it is an hegge hogge. Thus he chasyth and wote not what. He comyth home at euyn rayn beten pryckyd: and his clothes torn wete shode all myry. Some hounde loste: some surbat. Suche greues and many other hapyth vnto the hunter, whyche for dyspleysaunce of theym y^t loue it I dare not reporte. Thus truly me semyth that this is not the beste dysporte and game of the sayd foure. The dysporte and game of hawkynge is laboryous and noyouse also as me semyth. For often the fawkener loseth his hawkes as the hunter his houndes. Thenne is his game and his dysporte goon. Full often cryeth he and whystelyth tyll that he be ryght euyll a thurste. His hawke taketh a bowe and lyste not ones on hym rewarde. whan he wolde haue her for to flee: thenne woll she bathe. with mys fedynge she shall haue the Fronse: the Rye: the Cray and many other

syknesses that brynge theym to the Sowse. Thus
by prouff this is not the beste dysporte and game
of the sayd foure. The dysporte and game of
fowlynge me semyth moost symple. For in the
wynter season the fowler spedyth not but in the
moost hardest and coldest weder: whyche is
greuous: For whan he wolde goo to his gynnes he
may not for colde. Many a gynne and many a
snare he makyth. Yet soryly dooth he fare. At
morn tyde in the dewe he is weete shode vnto
his taylle. Many other suche I could tell: but
drede of magre makith me for to leue. Thus
me semeth that huntynge and hawkynge and
also fowlynge ben so laborous and greuous that
none of theym maye perfourme nor bi very meane
that enduce a man to a mery spyryte: whyche is
cause of his longe lyfe acordynge unto ye sayd
parable of Salamon. Dowteles thenne foloweth
it that it must nedes be the dysporte of fysshynge
wyth an angle. For all other manere of fysshyng
is also laborous and greuous: often makynge folkes
ful wete and colde, whyche many tymes hath
been cause of grete Infirmytees. But the angler
may have no colde nor no dysease nor angre, but
yf he be causer hymself. For he maye not lese at
the moost but a lyne or an hoke: of whiche he
maye haue store plentie of his owne makynge, as
this symple treatyse shall teche hym. Soo thenne
his losse is not greuous. and other greyffes maye he

not haue, sauynge but yf ony fisshe breke away after that he is take on the hoke; or elles that he catche nought: whyche ben not greuous. For yf he faylle of one he maye not faylle of a nother, yf he dooth as this treatyse techyth; but yf there be nought in the water. And yet atte the leest he hath his holsom walk and mery at his ease. a swete ayre of the swete sauoure of the meede floures: that makyth hym hungry. He hereth the melodyous armony of fowles. He seeth the yonge swannes: heerons: duckes: cotes and many other foules wyth theyr brodes. whyche me semyth better than alle the noyse of houndys: the blastes of hornys and the scrye of foulis that hunters: fawkeners and fowlers can make. And yf the angler take fysshe: surely thenne is there noo man merier than he is in his spyryte. Also who soo woll vse the game of anglynge: he must ryse erly. whiche thyng is prouffytable to man in this wyse: That is to wyte: moost to the heele of his soule. For it shall cause hym to be holy. and to the heele of his body. For it shall cause hym to be hole. Also to the encrease of his goodys. For it shall make hym ryche. As the olde englysshe prouerbe sayth in this wyse. (who so woll ryse erly shall be holy helthy and zely.) Thus haue I prouyd in myn entent that the dysporte and game of anglynge is the very meane and cause that enducith a man in to a mery spyryte. Whyche after the

sayde parable of Salomon and the sayd
doctryne of phisyk makyth a flouryng aege and a
longe. And therfore to al you that ben vertuous:
gentyll: and free borne I wryte and make this
symple treatyse folowynge: by whyche ye may
haue the full crafte of anglynge to dysport you at
your luste: to the entent that your aege maye the
more floure and the more lenger to endure.

YF ye woll be crafty in anglynge: ye must fyrst
lerne to make your harnays. That is to wyte
your rodde: your lynes of dyuers colours. After
that ye must know how ye shall angle in what
place of the water: how depe: and what time of
day. For what manere of fysshe: in what wedyr
How many impedymentes there ben in fysshynge
y^t is callyd anglynge And in specyall wyth what
baytys to euery dyuers fysshe in eche moneth of
the yere. How ye shall make your baytes brede
where ye shall fynde theym: and how ye shall
kepe theym. And for the moost crafty thynge
how ye shall make youre hokes of stele and of
osmonde, Some for the dubbe; and some for the
flote: and the grounde, as ye shall here after al
thyse fynde expressed openly vnto your knowlege.

And how ye shall make your rodde craftly here
I shall teche you. Ye shall kytte betwene

Myghelmas and Candylmas a fayr staffe of a fadom and a halfe longe: and arme grete of hasyll: wylowe; or aspe. And bethe hym in an hote owyn: and sette hym euyn. Thenne lete hym cole and drye a moneth. Take thenne and frette hym faste wyth a cockeshotecorde: and bynde hym to a fourme or an euyn square grete tree. Take thenne a plummers wire that is euyn and streyte and sharpe at the one ende. And hete the sharpe ende in a charcole fyre tyll it be whyte: and brenne the staffe therwyth thorugh: euer streyte in the pythe at bothe endes tyll they mete. And after that brenne hym in the nether ende wyth a byrde broche, and wyth other broches eche gretter than other. and euer the grettest the laste: so that ye make your hole aye tapre were. Thenne lete hym lye still and kele two dayes. Vnfrette hym thenne and lete hym drye in an hous roof in the smoke tyll he be thrugh drye. In the same season take a fayr yerde of grene hasyll and beth hym euyn rnd streyghte. and lete it drye with the staffe. And whan they ben drye make the yerde mete vnto the hole in the staffe: vnto halfe the length of the staffe. And to perfourme that other halfe of the croppe. Take a fayr shote of blacke thornn: crabbe tree: medeler. or of Ienypre kytte in the same season: and well bethyd and streyghte. And frette theym togyder fetely: soo that the croppe maye iustly

8 TREATYSE OF FYSSHYNGE.

entre all in to the sayd hole. Thenne shaue your staffe wexe. Thenne vyrell the staffe at bothe endes wyth longe hopis of yren or laton in the clennest wyse wyth a pike in the nether ende fastnyd wyth a rennynge vyce: to take in and out your croppe. Thenne set your croppe an handfull within the ouer ende of your staffe in suche wise that it be as bigge there as in ony other place aboue. Thenne arme your croppe at thouer ende downe to ye frette wyth a lyne of. vj. heeres. And dubbe the lyne and frette it fast in ye toppe wyth a bowe to fasten on your lyne. And thus shall ye make you a rodde soo preuy that ye maye walke therwyth: and there shall noo man wyte where abowte yee goo. It woll be lyghte and full nymbyll to fysshe with at your luste. And for the more redynesse loohere a fygure therof in example:*

AFTER that ye haue made thus your rodde: ye must lerne to coloure your lynes of here in this wyse. Firste ye must take of a whyte horse taylle the lengest heere and fayrest that ye can finde. And euer the rounder it be the better it is. Departe it in to. vj. partes: and euery parte ye

---

* In the original here follows a rude diagram representing a rod.

shall colour by hymselfe in dyuers colours. As yelowe: grene: browne: tawney: russet: and duske colours. And for to make a good grene colour on your heer ye shall doo thus. Take small ale a quarte and put it in a lytyll panne: and put therto halfe a pounde of alym. And put therto your heer: and lete it boylle softly half an houre. Thenne take out your heer: and let it drye. Thenne take a potell of water and put it in a panne. And put therin two handfull of ooldys or of wyxen. And presse it wyth a tyle stone: and lete it boylle solftly half an houre. And whan it is yelow on the scume put therin your heer wyth halfe a pounde of coparose betyn in powdre and lete it boylle halfe a myle waye: and thenne sette it downe: and lete it kele fyue or fyxe houres. Thenne take out the heer and drye it. And it is thenne the fynest grene that is for the water. And euer the more ye put therto of coparose the better it is. or elles in stede of it vertgrees.

A nother wyse ye maye make more bryghter grene, as thus sete woode your heer in an woode-fatte a lyght plunket colour. And thenne sethe hym in olde or wyxin lyke as I haue sayd sauynge ye shall not put therto neyther coporose ne vertgrees.

For to make your heer yelow dyght it wyth alym as I haue sayd before. And after that wyth oldys or wyxin wythout coporose or vertgrees. A nother yelow ye shall make thus. Take smalle ale a potell: and stampe thre handful of walnot leues and put togider: And put in your heer tyll that it be as depe as ye woll haue it. For to make russet heer. Take stronge lye a pynt and halfe a pounde of sote and a lytyl iuce of walnot leuys and a quarte of alym: and put theym alle togydder in a panne and boylle theym well. And whan it is colde put in youre heer tyll it be as derke as ye woll haue it. For to make a browne colour. Take a pounde of sote and a quarte of ale: and seth it wyth as many walnot leuys as ye maye. And whan they wexe blacke sette it from the fire. And put therin your heer and lete it lye styll tyll it be as browne as ye woll haue it.

For to make a nother browne. Take strong ale and sote and tempre them togyder. and put therin your heer two dayes and two nyghtes and it shall be ryght a good colour.

For to make a tawney coloure. Take lyme and water and put theym togyder: and also put your heer therin foure or fyue houres. Thenne take it out and put it in a Tanners ose a day: and it shall be also fyne a tawney colour as nedyth to our purpoos. The syrte parte of your heer ye shall kepe styll whyte for lynes for the dubbyd hoke to fysshe for the trought and graylynge and for smalle lynes for to trye for the roche and the darse.

WHAN your heer is thus colourid: ye must knowe for whiche waters and for whyche seasons they shall serue.

The grene colour in all clere water from Apryll tyll Septembre. The yelowe coloure in euery clere water from Septembre tyll Nouembre: For is is lyke ye wedys and other manere grasse which growyth in the waters and ryuers whan they ben broken. The russet colour seruyth all the wynter vnto the ende of Apryll, as well in ryuers as in poles or lakys. The browne colour seruyth for that water that is blacke dedisshe in ryuers or in other waters. The tawney colour for those waters that ben hethy or morysshe.

NOW must ye make youre lynes in this wyse. Fyrste loke that ye haue an Instrument lyke vnto this fygure portrayed folowynge. Thenne take your heer and kytte of the smalle ende an hondfull large or more, For it is neyther stronge nor yet sure. Thenne torne the toppe to the taylle eueryche ylyke moche. And departe it into thre partyes. Thenne knytte euery part at the one ende by hymself. And at the other ende knytte till thre togyder: and put ye same ende in that other ende of your Instrument that hath but one clyft. And sett that other ende faste wyth the **wegge** foure fyngers in alle shorter than your heer. Thenne twyne euery warpe one waye and ylyke moche: and fasten theym in thre clystes ylyke streyghte. Take thenne out that other ende and twyne it that waye that it woll desyre ynough. Thenne streyne it a lytyll: and knytte it for ondoynge: and that is good. And for to knowe to make your Instrument: loo here it is in fygure. And it shall be made of tree sauynge the bolte vnderneth: whiche shall be of yren.*

WHAN ye haue as many of the lynkys as ye suppose wol suffyce for the length of a lyne: then must ye knytte theym togyder wyth a water knotte or elles a duchys knotte. And whan your knotte is knytte: kytte of ye voyde shorte endes a strawe brede from the knotte. Thus shal ye make youre lynes fayr and fyne: and also ryght sure for ony manere fysshe. And by cause that ye sholde knowe bothe the water knotte and also the duchys knotte: loo theym here in fygure caste vnto the lyknesse of the draughte.

YE shall vnderstonde that the moost subtyll and hardyste crafte in makynge of your harnays is for to make your hokis. For whoos makyng ye must haue fete fyles. thynn and sharpe and smalle beten: A semy clamm of yren: a bender

---

* In the original here follows a rude diagram.

a payr of longe and smalle tongys: an harde knyfe somdeale thycke: an anuelde: and a lytyll hamour. And for smalle fysshe ye shall make your hokes of the smallest quarell nedlys that ye can fynde of stele, and in this wyse. Ye shall put the quarell in a redde charkcolefyre tyll that it be of the same colour that the fyre is. Thenne take hym out and lete hym kele: and ye shal fynde him well alayd for to fyle. Thenne reyse the herde wyth your knyfe, and make the poynt sharpe. Thenne alaye hym agayn: for elles he woll breke in the bendyng. Thenne bende hym lyke to the bende fyguryd herafter in example. And gretter hokes ye shall make in the same wyse of gretter nedles: as broderers nedlis: or taylers: or shomakers nedlis spere poyntes and of shomakers nalles, in especyall the beste for grete fysshe. and that they bende atte the poynt whan they ben assayed, for elles they ben not good. Whan the hoke is bendyd bete the hynder ende abrode: and fyle it smothe for fretynge of thy lyne. Thenne sodaynly quenche it in water: and it woll be harde and stronge. And for to haue knowlege of your Instrumentes: lo theym here in fygure portrayd.*

---

* In the original here follow rude diagrams representing hooks.

WHAN ye haue made thus your hokis: thenne must ye set theym on your lynes acordynge in gretnesse and strength in this wyse. Ye shal take smalle redde silke. and yf it be for a grete hoke thenne double it: not twynyd. And elles for small hokys lete it be syngle: and therwyth frette thycke the lyne there as the one ende of your hoke shal sytte a strawe brede. Thenne sette there your hoke: and frette hym wyth the same threde ye two partes of the lengthe that shall be frette in all. And whan ye come to the thyrde parte thenne torne the ende of your lyne agayn vpon the frette double. and frette it so double that other thyrde part. Thenne put your threde in at the hose twys or thries and let it goo at eche tyme rounde abowte the yerde of your hoke. Thenne wete the hose and drawe it tyll that it be faste. And loke that your lyne lye euermore wythin your hokys: and not without. Thenne kytte of the lynys ende and the threde as nyghe as ye maye: sauynge the frette.

NOW ye knowe wyth how grete hokys ye shall angle to euery fysshe; now I woll tell you wyth how many heeres ye shall to euery manere of fisshe. For the menow wyth a lyne of one heere. For the waxyng roche. the blecke and the gogyn and the ruffe wyth a lyne of two heeris. For the darse and the grete roche with a lyne of thre heeres. For the perche: the flounder and bremet with foure heeres. For the cheuen chubbe: the breme. the tenche and the ele wyth. vj heeres. For the troughte: graylynge: barbyll and the grete chewyn wyth. ix. heeres. For the grete troughte wyth. xii. heeres. For the samon wyth. xv. heeres. And for the pyke wyth a chalke lyne made browne with your browne colour aforsayd: arrayd with a wyre. as ye shall here herafter whan I speke of the pyke.

Your lynes must be plumbid wyth lede. And ye shall wyte y^t the nexte plumbe vnto the hoke shall be therfro a large fote and more. And euery plumbe of a quantyte to the gretnes of the lyne. There be thre manere of plumbis for a grounde lyne rennynge. And for the flote set upon the grounde lyne lyenge. x. plumbes joynynge all togider to the grounde lyne rennynge. ix or x. smalle. The flote plumbe shall be so heuy y^t the leest plucke of ony fysshe maye pull it downe in to ye water. And make your plumbis rounde and smothe y^t they stycke not on stonys or on wedys. And for the more vnderstondynge lo theym here in fygure.*

---

* In the original here follow rude diagrams representing the leads.

THENNE shall ye make your flotys in this wyse. Take a fayr corke that is clene without many holes. and bore it thrugh wyth a smalle hote yren: And putt therin a penne luste and streyghte. Euer the more flote the gretter penne and greter hole. Then shape it grete in the myddis and small at bothe endys. and specyally sharpe in the nether ende, and lyke vnto the the fygures folowynge. And make theym smothe on a gryndyng stone: or on a tyle stone. And loke that the flote for one heer be no more than a pese. For two heeres: as a beene for twelue heeres: as a walnot. And soo euery lyne after the proporcion. All manere lynes that be not for the grounde must have flotes. And the rennynge grounde lyne must haue a flote. The lyenge grounde lyne wythout flote.*

NOW I haue lernyd you to make all your harnays. Here I woll tell you how ye shall angle. Ye shall angle: vnderstande that there is. vj. manere of anglyng. That one is at the grounde for the troughte and other fisshe. A nother is at ye grounde at an arche, or at a stange where it ebbyth and flowyth: for bleke: roche: and darse. The thyrde is wyth a flote for all

---

* In the original here follow rude diagrams representing the floats.

manere of fysshe. The fourth wyth a menow for yᵉ troughte wythout plumbe or flote The fyfth is rennynge in yᵉ same wyse for roche and darse wyth one or two heeres and a flye. The syxte is wyth a dubbyd hoke for the troughte and graylyng. And for the fyrste and pryncypall poynt in anglynge: kepe yᵉ euer fro the water fro the syghte of the fysshe: other wyse kneele on the londe: or ellys behynde a busshe that the fysshe se you not. For yf they doo they wol not byte. Also loke that ye shadow not the water as moche as ye may. For it is that thynge that woll soone fraye the fysshe. And yf a fysshe be afrayed he woll not bite longe after. For alle manere fysshe that fede by the grounde ye shall angle for theym to the botom. Soo that your hokys shall renne or lye on the grounde, And for alle other fysshe that fede aboue ye shall angle to theym in the myddes of the water or somdeale byneth or somdeale aboue. For euer the gretter fysshe ther nerer he lyeth the botom of the water. And euer the smaller fysshe the more he swymmyth aboue. The thyrde good poynt is whan the fysshe bytyth that ye be not to hasty to smyte nor to late, For ye must abide tyll ye suppose that the bayte be toke in the mouth of the fysshe, and thenne abyde noo longer. And this is for the grounde. And for the flote whan ye se it pullyd softly vnder the water: or elles caryed vpon the water softly:

thenne smyte. And loke that ye neuer ouer-smyte the strengthe of your lyne for brekynge. And yf it fortune you to smyte a grete fysshe wyth a smalle harnays: thenne ye must lede hym in the water and labour hym there tyll he be drownyd and ouercome. Thenne take hym as well as ye can or maye. and euer bewaar that ye holde not ouer the strengthe of your lyne. And as moche as ye may lete hym not come out of your lynes ende streyghte from you: But kepe hym euer vnder the rodde, and euermore holde hym streyghte: soo that your lyne may susteyne and beere his lepys and his plungys wyth the helpe of your croppe and of your honde.

HERE I woll declare vnto you in what place of the water ye shall angle. Ye shall angle in a pole or in a stondinge water in euery place where it is ony thynge depe. There is not grete choyse of ony places where it is ony thynge depe in a pole. For it is but a pryson to fysshe and they lyue for ye more parte in hungre lyke prisoners: and therfore it is the lesse maystry to take theym. But in a ryuer ye shall angle in euery place where it is depe and clere by the grounde: as grauell or claye wythout mudde or wedys. And in espe-cyall yf that there be a manere whyrlynge of water or a couert. As an holow-banke: or grete rotys of trees: or longe wedes flotyng aboue in the water where the fysshe may couere and hyde theymself at certayn tymes whan they lyste. Also it is good for to angle styffe stremys and also in fallys of waters and weares: and in floode gatys and mylle pyttes, And it is good for to angle where as the water restyth by the banke: and where the streme rennyth nyghe thereby: and is depe and clere by the grounde and mony other placys where ye may se any fyssh houe or haue ony fedynge.

NOW we shall wyte what tyme of the daye ye shall angle From the begynnynge of May vntyll it be Septembre the mornynge tyme is erly by the morowe from foure of ye clocke vnto eyghte of the clocke: And at after none from foure of the clock vnto eyghte of the clocke: but not soo good as in the mornynge. And yf it be a colde whystelyng wynde and a derke lowrynge daye. For a derke daye is moche better to angle in than a clere daye. From the begynnynge of Septembre vnto the ende of Apryll spare noo tyme of the daye:

Also many pole fysshes woll byte in the nonetyde.

And yf ye se ony tyme of the daye the trought or graylynge lepe: angle to hym wyth a dubbe acordynge to the same month. And where the water ebbyth and flowyth the fysshe woll byte in some place at the ebbe: and in some place at the flood. After y^t they haue restynge behynde stangnys and archys of brydgys and other suche maner places.

HERE ye shall wyte in what weder ye shall angle. as I sayd before in a derke lowrynge daye whanne the wynde blowyth softly. And in somer season whan it is brennynge hote it is nought. From Septembre vnto Apryll in a fayr sonny daye is ryght good to angle. And yf the wynde in that season haue ony parte of the Oryent: the wedyr thenne is nought. And whan it is a grete wynde. And whan it snowith reynyth or hayllyth, or is a grete tempeste, as thondyr or lightenynge: or a swoly hote weder: thenne it is noughte for to angle.

NOW shall ye wyte that there ben twelue manere of ympedymentes whyche cause a man to take noo fysshe. w^t other corayn that maye casuelly happe. The fyrst is yf your harnays be not mete nor fetly made. The seconde is yf your baytes be not good nor fyne. The thyrde is yf that ye angle not in bytynge tyme. The fourth is yf that the fysshe be frayed w^t the syghte of a man. The fyfth yf the water be very thycke: whyte or redde of ony floode late fallen The syxte yf the fysshe moue not for colde. The seuenth yf that the wedyr be hote. The eyght yf it rayne. The nynthe yf it hayll or snow talle. The tenth is yf it be a tempeste. The eleuenth is yf it be a grete wynde. The twelfyfth yf the wynde be in the East, and that is worste For comynly neyther wynter nor somer ye fisshe woll not byte thenne. The weste and northe wyndes ben good but the south is beste.

And now I haue tolde you how to make your harnays: and how ye shall fisshe therwyth in al poyntes. Reason woll that ye knowe wyth what baytes ye shall angle to euery manere of fysshe in euery moneth of the yere, whyche is all the effecte of the crafte. And wythout whyche baytes knowen well by you all your other crafte here to form auayllyth you not to purpose. For ye can not brynge an hoke in to a fyssh mouth wythout a bayte. Which baytes for euery manere of fyssh and for euery moneth here folowyth in this wyse.

FOR by cause that the Samon is the moost stately fyssh that ony man maye angle to in fresshe water. Therfore I purpose to begynne at hym. The samon is a gentyll fysshe: but he is comborous for to take. For comynly he is best in depe places of grete ryuers: And for the more parte he holdyth the myddys of it: that a man maye not come at hym. And he is in season from Marche unto Myghelmas. In wyche season ye shall angle to hym wyth thyse baytes whan ye maye gete theym. Fyrste wyth a redde worme in the begynnynge and endynge of the season. And also wyth a bobbe that bredyth in a dunghyll. And specyally wyth a souerayn bayte that bredyth on a water docke. And he bytith not at the grounde: but at ye flote. Also ye may take hym but it is seldom seen with a dubbe at such tyme as whan he lepith in lyke fourme and manere as ye doo take a troughte or a graylynge. And thyse baytes ben well prouyd baytes for the samon.

THE Troughte for by cause he is a right deyntous fyssh and also a ryght feruente-byter we shall speke nexte of hym. He is in season fro Marche vnto Myghelmas. He is on clene grauely grounde and in a streme. Ye may angle to hym all tymes wyth a grounde lyne lyenge or rennynge; sauyng in lepynge tyme. and thenne wyth a dubbe. And erly wyth a rennynge grounde lyne. and forth in the daye wyth a flote lyne.

Ye shall angle to hym in Marche wyth a menew hangyd on your hoke by the nether nesse wythout flote or plumbe: drawynge vp and downe in the streme tyll ye fele hym taste. In the same tyme angle to hym wyth a grounde lyne with a redde worme for the moost sure. In Aprill take the same baytes: and also Iuneba other wyse namyd. ii. eyes. Also the canker that bredyth in a grete tree and the redde snayll. In May take yᵉ stone flye and the bobbe vnder the cowe torde and the sylke worme: and the bayte that bredyth on a fernne leyf. In Iuyn take a redde worme and nyppe of the heed: and put on thyn hoke a codworme byforn. In Iuyll take the grete redde worme and the codworme togyder. In August take a flesshe flye and the grete redde worme and the fatte of the bakon: and bynde abowte thy hoke. In Septembre take the redde worme and the menew. In Octobre take the same: for they ben specyall for the trought all tymes of the yere. From Aprill tyll Septembre yᵉ trought lepyth. thenne angle to hym wyth a dubbyd hoke acordynge to the moneth, whyche dubbyd hokys ye shall fynde in thende of this treatyse: and the monethys wyth theym.*

The grayllynge by a nother name callyd vmbre is a delycyous fysshe to mannys mouthe. And ye maye take hym lyke as ye doo the trought. And thyse ben his baytes. In Marche and in Apryll the redde worme. In Maye the grene worme: a lytyll breyled worme: the docke canker and the hawthorn worme. In Iune the bayte that bredyth betwene the tree and the barke of an oke. In Iuyll a bayte that bredyth on a fernne leyf: and the

---

* This has reference to a rude sketch of hooks at the end of the original.

grete redde worme. And nyppe of the hede: and put on your hoke a cod worme before. In August the redde worme: and a docke worme. And al the yere after a redde worme.

THE barbyll is a swete fysshe but it is a quasy meete and a peryllous for mannys body. For comynly he yeuyth an introduxion to ye Febres. And yf he be eten rawe: he maye be cause of mannys dethe: whyche hath oft be seen. Thyse be his baytes In Marche and in Apryll take fayr fresshe chese: and laye it on a borde and kytte it in small square pecys of the lengthe of your hoke. Take thenne a candyl and brenne it on the ende at the poynt of your hoke tyll it be yelow. And thenne bynde it on your hoke with fletchers sylke: and make it rough lyke a welbede. This bayte is good all the somer season. In May and Iune take ye hawthornne worme togyder. Also the water docke leyf worme and the hornet worme togyder. In Augusst and for all the yere take the talowe of a shepe and softe chese: of eche ylyke moche: and a lytyll hony and grynde or stampe theym togyder londe and tempre ittyll it be tough. And put therto floure a lytyll and make it on small pelletys. And y^t is a good bayte to angle wyth at the grounde. And loke that it synke in the water. or ellys it is not good to this purpoos.

THE carpe is a deyntous fysshe: but there ben but fewe in Englonde. And therfore I wryte the lasse of hym. He is an euyll fysshe to take. For he is soo stronge enarmyd in the mouthe that there maye noo weke harnays holde hym. And as touchynge his baytes I haue but lytyll knowlege of it. And me were loth to wryte more than I knowe and heue prouyd. But well I wote that the redde worme and the menow ben good baytes for hym at all tymes as I haue herde saye of persones credyble and also founde wryten in bokes of credence.

THE cheuyn is a stately fysshe and his heed is a deynty morsell. There is noo fysshe soo strongly enarmyd wyth scalys on the body. And bi cause he is a stronge byter he hathe the more baytes, whiche ben thyse. In Marche the redde worme at the grounde: For comynly thenne he woll byte there at all tymes of ye yere yf he be ony thinge hungry. In Apryll the dyche canker that bredith in the tree. A worme that bredith betwene the rynde and the tree of an oke. The redde worme; and the yonge froghys whan the fete ben kyt of. Also the stone flye the bobbe vnder the cowe torde: the redde snaylle. In May ye bayte that bredyth on the osyer beddys and the docke canker togyder vpon your hoke. Also a bayte that bredyth on a fernne leyf: ye codworme and a bayte that bredyth on an hawthornn. And a bayte that bredyth on an oke leyſ and a sylke worme and a cod worme togyder In Iune take the creket and the dorre and also a red worme : the heed kytte of and a codworme before : and put theym on yᵉ hoke. Alſo a bayte in the osyer leyſ yonge frogghys the thre-fete kitte of by the body : and the fourth by the knee. The bayte on the hawthornne and the cod worme togyder and a grubbe that bredyth in a dunghyll : and a grete greshop. In Iuyll the greshop and the humbylbee in the medow. Also yonge bees and yonge hornettes. Also a grete brended flye that bredyth in pathes of medowes and the flye that is amonge pysmeers hyllys. In August take wortwormes and magotes vnto Myghelmas. In Septembre the redde worme : and also take the bayte whan ye may gete theym : that is to wyte ; Cherges : yonge myce not heeryd : and the honie combe.

The breeme is a noble fysshe and a deyntous. And ye shall angle for hym from Marche vnto August wyth a redde worme and thenne wyth a butter flye and a grene flye. and wyth a bayte that bredyth amonge grene rede : and a bayte that bredyth in the barke of a deed tree. And for bremettis : take maggotes. And fro that tyme forth all the yere after take the red worme : and in the ryuer browne breede. Moo baytes there ben but they ben not easy and therfore I lete theym passe over.

A TENCHE is a good fysshe: and heelith all manere of other fysshe that ben hurte yf they maye come to hym. He is the most parte of the year in the mudde. And he styryth moost in Iune and Iuly: and in other seasons but lytyll. He is an euyll byter. his baytes ben thyse. For all the yere browne breede tostyd wyth hony in lyknesse of a butterydloof: and the grete redde worme And as for cheyf take the black blood in ye herte of a shepe and floure and hony. And tempre theym all togyder somdeale softer than paast: and anoynt therwyth the redde worme: bothe for this fysshe and for other. And they woll byte moche the better therat at all tymes.

The perche is a daynteous fysshe and passynge holsom and a free bytyng. Thise ben his baytes. In Marche the redde worme. In Aprill the bobbe vnder the cowe torde. In May the slothornn worme and the codworme. In Iune the bayte that bredith in an olde fallen oke and the great canker In Iuyll the bayte that bredyth on the osyer leyf and the bobbe that bredyth on the dunghyll: and the hawthornn worme and the cod worme. In August the redde worme and maggotes. All the yere after the red worme as for the beste.

The roche is an easy fysshe to take. And yf he be fatte and pennyd thenne is he good meete, and thyse ben his baytes. In Marche the most redy bayte is the red worme. In Apryll the bobbe vnder the cowe torde. In May the bayte y^t bredyth on ye oke leyſ and the bobbe in the dunghyll. In Iune the bayte that bredyth on the osyer and the cod worme. In Iuyll hous flyes. and the bayte that bredith on an oke. and the not worme and maggotes tyll Myghelmas. And after y^t the ſatte of bakon.

The dace is a genryll fysshe to take. and yſ it he well reset thenne is it good meete. In Marche his bayte is a redde worme. In Apryll the bobbe vnder the cowe torde. In May the docke canker and the bayte on ye flothornn and on the oken leyſ. In Iune the codworme and the bayte on the osyer and the whyte grubbe in ye dunghyll. In Iuyll take hous flyes and flyes that brede in pysmer hylles: the codworme and maggotes vnto Mighelmas. And yſ the water be clere ye shall take fysshe whan other take none. And fro that time forth doo as ye do for the roche. For comynly theyr bytynge and their baytes ben lyke.

The bleke is but a feble fysshe. yet he is holsom. His baytes from Marche to Myghelmas be the same that I haue wryten before. For the roche and darse sauynge all the somer season asmoche as ye maye angle for hym wyth an house flye: and in wynter season w^t bakon and other bayte made as ye herafter may know.

The ruf is ryght an holsom fysshe: And ye shall angle to him wyth the same baytes in al seasons of the yere and in the same wise as I haue tolde you of the perche: for they ben lyke in fysshe and fedinge, sauynge the ruf is lesse. And therfore he must haue ye smaller bayte.

The flounder is an holsom fisshe and a free. And a subtyll byter in his manere. For comynly whan he soukyth his meete he fedyth at grounde. and therfore ye must angle to hym wyth a grounde lyne lyenge. And he hath but one manere of bayte. and that is a red worme. whiche is moost cheyf for all manere of fysshe. The gogen is a good fisshe: and he byteth wel at the grounde: And his baytes for all the yere ben thyse. ye red worme: codworme: and maggotes. And ye must angle to him wt a flote. and lete your bayte be nere ye botom or ellis on ye grounde.

The menow whan he shynith in the water thenne is he bytyr. And though his body be lytyll yet he is a rauenous biter and an egre. And ye shall angle to hym wyth the same baytes that ye doo for the gogyn: sauynge they must be smalle.

The ele is a quasy fysshe a rauenous and deuourer of the brode of fysshe. And for the pyke also is a deuourer of fysshe I put them bothe behynde all other to angle. For this ele ye shall finde an hole in the grounde of the water, and it is blewe blackysshe there put in your hoke tyll that it be a fote wythin ye hole, and your bayte shall be a grete angyll twytch or a menow.

The pyke is a good fysshe: but for he deuouryth so many as well of his owne kynde as of other: I loue hym the lesse. and for to take hym ye shall doo thus. Take a codlynge hoke: and take a roche or a fresshe heering and a wyre wyth an hole in the ende: and put it in at the mouth and out at the taylle downe by the ridge of the fresshe heeryng. And then put the lyne of your hoke in after. and drawe the hoke into the cheke of ye fresshe heeryng. Thenne put a plumbe of lede upon your lyne a yerde longe from youre hoke and a flote in mydwaye betwene: and caste it in a pyrte where the pyke vsyth. And this is the beste and moost surest crafte of takynge the pyke. A nother manere takynge of hym there is. Take a frogghe and put it on your hoke at the necke bytwene the skynne and the body on ye backe half: and put on a flote a yerde therfro: and caste it where the pyke hauntyth and ye shall haue hym. Another manere. Take the same bayte and put it in Asafetida and cast it in the water with a corde and a corke: and ye shall not fayll of hym. And yf ye lyst to haue a good sporte: thenne tye the corde to a gose fote: and ye shall se god halynge whether the gose or the pyke shall haue the better.

NOW ye wote with what baytes and how ye shall angle to euery manere fysshe. Now I woll tell you how ye shall kepe and fede you quycke baytes. Ye shall fede and kepe them all in generall: but euery manere by hymselfe wyth suche thyng, in and on whiche they brede. And as longe as they ben quycke and newe they ben fyne. But whan they ben in a slough or elles deed then ben they nought. Oute of thyse ben excepted thre brodes: That is to wyte of hornettys: humbylbees. and waspys. whom ye shall bake in breede and after dyppe theyr heedes in blode and lete theym drye. Also excepte maggotes: whyche whan thei ben bredde grete wyth theyr naturell fedynge: ye shall fede theym ferthermore wyth shepes talow and wyth a cake made of floure and hony. thenne woll they be more grete. And whan ye haue clensyd theym wyth sonde in a bagge of blanket kepte hote vnder your gowne or other warmm thyng two hours or thre. thenne ben they beste and redy to angle wyth. And of the frogghe kytte y ͤ legge by the knee. of the grasshop the leggys and wynges by the body.

Thyse ben baytes made to last all the yere. Fyrste been floure and lene flesshe of the hepis of a cony or of a catte: virgyn wexe and shepys talowe: and braye theym in a morter: And thenne tempre it at the fyre wyth a lytyll puryfyed hony: and soo make it vp in lytyll ballys and bayte therwyth your hokys after theyr quantyte. and this is a good bayte for all maner fresshe fysshe.

A nother: take the sewer of a shepe and chese in lyke quantyte: aud braye theim togider longe in a mortere. And take thenne floure and tempre it therwyth. and after that alaye it wyth hony and make ballys therof. and that is for the barbyll in especyall.

A nother for darse and roche, and bleke. take whete and sethe it well and thenne put it in blood all a daye and a nyghte. and it is a good bayte.

For baytes for grete fyssh kepe specyally this rule. Whan ye haue take a grete fysshe: vndo the mawe. and what ye fynde therin make that your bayte: for it is beste.

Thyse ben the xii. flyes with whyche ye shall angle to ye trought and grayllyng and dubbe lyke as ye shall now here me tell.

Marche.

THE donne flye the body of the donne woll and the wyngis of the pertryche. A nother doone flye: the body of blacke woll: the wynges of the blackest drake: and the Iay vnder the wynge and vnder the tayle.

Apryll.

The stone flye. the bodye of blacke wull: and yelowe vnder the wynge. and vnder the tayle and the wynges of the drake. In the begynnynge of May a good flye. the body of roddyd wull and lappid abowte wyth blacke sylke: the wynges of the drake and of the redde capons hakyll.

May.

The yelow flye. the body of yelow wull: the wynges of the redde cocke hakyll and of the drake lyttyd below. The blacke louper. the body of blacke wull and lappyd abowte wyth the herle of ye pecok tayle: and the wynges of ye redde capon w^t a blewe heed.

June.

The donne cutte: the body of blacke wull and a yelow lyste after eyther syde: the wynges of the bosarde bounde on with barkyd hempe. The maure flye. the body of dolke wull the wynges of the blackest mayle of the wylde drake. The taudy flye at saynt Wyllyams daye. the body of taudy wull and the wynges contrary eyther ayenst other of the whitest mayle of ye wylde drake.

Juyll.

The waspe flye. the body of blacke wull and lappid abowte w^t yelow threde: the winges of the bosarde. The shell flye at saynt Thomas daye. the body of grene wull and lappyd abowte wyth the herle of the pecoks tayle: wynges of the bosarde.

August.

The drake flye. the body of blacke wull and lappid abowte wyth blacke sylke: wynges of the mayle of the blacke drake wyth a blacke heed.

Thyse fygures are put in here in ensample of your hokes.*

Here folowyth the order made to all those whiche shall haue the vnderstondynge of this forsayde treatyse and vse it for theyr pleasures.

YE that can angle and take fysshe to your plesures as this forsayd treatyse techyth and shewyth you: I charge and requyre you in the name of alle noble men that ye fysshe not in noo poore mannys seuerall water; as his ponde: stewe: or other necessary thynges to kepe fysshe in wythout his lycence and good wyll. Nor that ye vse not to breke noo mannys gynnys lyenge in theyr weares and in other places due vnto thym. Ne to take the fysshe awaye that is taken in theym. For after a fysshe is taken in a mannys gynne yf the gynne be layed in the comyn waters: or elles in suche waters as he hireth, it is his owne propre goodes. And yf ye take it awaye ye robbe

---

* In the original here follow rude diagrams representing the above hooks.

hym: wyche is a ryght shamfull dede to ony noble man to do and that theuys and brybours done: whyche are punysshed for theyr euyll dedes by the necke and otherwyse whan they maye be aspyed and taken. And also yf ye doo in lyke manere as this treatise shewyth you: ye shal haue no nede to take of other mennys: whiles ye shal haue ynough of your owne takyng yf ye lyste to labour therfore. whych shall be to you a uery pleasure to see the fayr bryght shynynge scalyd fysshes dysceyued by your crafty meanes and drawn vpon londe. Also that ye breke noo mannys heggys in goynge abowte your dysportes: ne opyn noo mannes gates but that ye shytte theym agayn. Also ye shall not vse this forsayd crafty dysporte for no couetysenes to thencreasynge and sparynge of your money oonly. but pryncypally for your solace and to cause the helthe of your body, and specyally of your soule. For whanne ye purpoos to goo on your disportes in fysshyng ye woll not desyre gretly many persones wyth you. whiche myghte lette you of your game. And thenne ye maye serue god deuowtly in sayenge affectuously youre custumable prayer. And thus doynge ye shall eschewe and voyde many vices. as ydylnes whyche is pryncypall cause in enduce man to many other vyces as it is ryght well knowen. Also ye shall not be to rauenous in takyng of your sayd game as to moche at one tyme. which ye maye lyghtly doo yf ye doo in euery poynt as this present treaty shewyth you in euery poynt. whiche sholde lyghtly be occasyon to dystroye your owne dysportes and other mannys also. As whan ye haue a sufycyent mete ye sholde coueyte no more as at that tyme. Also ye shall besye yourselfe to nourryssh the game in all that ye may: and to dysporte all suche thynges as ben deuourers of it. And all those that done after this rule shall haue the blessynge of god and saynt Peter, whyche he theym graunte that wyth his precyous blood vs boughte.

And for by cause that this present treatyse sholde not come to the hondys of eche persone whyche wolde desire it yf it were empryntyd allone by itself and put in a lytyll plaunflet therfore I* haue compyled it in a greter volume of dyuerse bokys concernynge to gentyll and noble men to the entent that the forsayd persones whyche sholde haue but lytyll mesure in the sayd dysporte of fysshyng sholde not by this meane vtterly dystroye it.

---

* These words are Wynkyn de Worde's, on adding the Treatyse of Fysshynge to the second edition of the Boke of St. Albans.

THE END.

Printed in Dunstable, United Kingdom